AF382196

HOW TO MAKE THE MOST OF YOUR PERFORMANCE APPRAISAL

Adopt a winning attitude and reap the benefits

Written by Caroline Cailteux
Translated by Emma Hanna

Coaching 50MINUTES.com

HOW TO MAKE THE MOST OF YOUR PERFORMANCE APPRAISAL

- **Problem:** how can I prepare for a performance appraisal, and what approach should I take in order to keep the discussion centred on constructive criticism for both manager and employee?
- **Uses:** evaluating results over a fixed time period and setting new objectives with the aim of improving employee skills and ensuring an atmosphere that is conducive to professional development.
- **Professional context:** management, human resource management, professional development.
- **FAQs:**
  - How frequently should performance appraisals be held?
  - How can I ensure that the atmosphere of the

meeting fosters communication and trust?
  ◦ Can I talk about anything during the meeting?
  ◦ How should I react to a negative performance appraisal?
  ◦ How should I handle an employee who reacts badly to any kind of criticism?
  ◦ How can I identify the obstacles to the goals set during the performance appraisal and help others to overcome them?

Although all employees must face a performance appraisal at some point, many approach it with dread; even its very name awakens our fear of being weighed and found wanting. However, this meeting is an opportunity for managers and employees to open a dialogue and, when properly managed, it can actually contribute to the company's development and to individual wellbeing.

So how can we prepare for a performance appraisal and ensure that it leaves us feeling satisfied and motivated? How can we create an atmosphere that fosters communication? How can we reassure employees and put them at ease so that they share and absorb the information that will help them to move forward and adopt new perspectives as they work? In just 50 minutes, you will discover the secrets to overcoming the trepidation associated with performance appraisals and turning the meeting into a constructive encounter. This short book has something to offer for anyone who has a role to play in this process: employers, managers, human resource managers, and of course, employees. The guidance provided here will help you to make the most of your performance appraisals, which are, at their core, a way for the human dimension of human resource management to come to the fore.

AN EFFECTIVE, STRESS-FREE PERFORMANCE APPRAISAL: THE BASICS

PERFORMANCE APPRAISALS: A COMPLEX SUPPORT MECHANISM

What are performance appraisals?

Performance appraisals are usually held once a year, and are an opportunity for human resource managers (or a colleague from the employee's department) and the employee in question to evaluate their work over a fixed period of time and to set progress goals for the future. This one-on-one meeting has several objectives:

- to define the expectations of the manager, the employee and the company's clients;
- to identify any problems that have been encountered by evaluating the achievements and actions of that period (in a constructive manner);

- to make a note of the progress that has been made, analyse the employee's strengths and weaknesses, evaluate their work, identify any necessary changes and sketch out their future prospects;
- to take stock of the employee's motivations and career;
- to identify the needs that must be met in order to motivate the employee and ensure their future progress, then formulate a development and training plan;
- to clarify any misunderstandings and restore a mutually beneficial relationship, if necessary.

Comments and notes on the employee's performance and abilities are recorded in an evaluation chart.

CAUTION

A performance appraisal should not be:

- a pretext for aggressive reprimands or settling a score;
- a trial – the employee should not feel as though they are being judged personally, and the human resource manager should

analyse the facts objectively;
- a monologue – the employee should be free to express their frustrations and discuss the difficulties they have faced with their manager;
- a source of stress; on the contrary, it should be a chance to grow.

The different types of appraisal

An employee evaluation is a complex process which should not be taken lightly. Managers should reflect on each meeting beforehand in order to identify the elements to be evaluated and an appropriate approach which will keep the meeting on track and ensure that the employee receives constructive feedback. In their book *Méthodologie du recueil d'informations* ("Methodology for Gathering Information"), the experts Jean-Marie de Ketele and Xavier Roegiers explain that the employer's goals and, by extension, their approach are determined by the nature of the decisions they expect to take based on the outcome of the appraisal (decisions to improve a process, whether or not to embark on a project, to offer a promotion, etc.). More broadly speaking, the two authors claim that appraisals can be focused on:

- **Orientation.** This often precedes action, and aims to evaluate whether or not the employee has taken the learning experiences of one stage on board before they move on to the next stage. During the appraisal, the person conducting the meeting will evaluate whether or not the employee is fit for their role by determining if they fulfil the position's requirements, or if they should be reassigned or receive further training. These appraisals focus on analysing the needs at hand and identifying the employee's strengths and weaknesses.
- **Regulation.** The goal of these appraisals is to gather useful information which can be used to improve performance. During the meeting, the employee and their manager work together to determine which actions should be taken to adjust the process. In this example, the manager will identify the strengths and weaknesses of the employee's role within the operational system, as well as the strategies that have been established.
- **Achievement.** These appraisals often take

place at the end of a project and determine whether it was a success or a failure. They focus on examining the results (whether they are positive or negative) and on an overview of the knowledge and skills acquired by the employee (noting whether or not they have been taken fully on board or not). During the appraisal, the manager or the human resource manager may decide to offer the employee a promotion or a permanent contract.

Types of appraisal	Subject for analysis	Questions to focus on during the meeting
Orientation appraisal	Resources	What are the necessary skills for this role?
Regulation appraisal	Process	Have adequate strategies been put in place to improve the employee's skills? Are adjustments necessary?
Achievement appraisal	Results	How can I praise the employee's successes and offer constructive feedback in case of failure?

Employee feedback can be given during all of these different types of appraisal. The approach to be taken should be chosen based on the objective of the appraisal, its importance and when it takes place.

Who conducts the appraisal?

The nature of the appraisal varies depending on the evaluator's role and position within the company. Appraisals can be carried out by:

- **The employee (self-evaluation).** The employee analyses their own strengths and weaknesses in order to then set their own goals. This approach fosters motivation, because the employee is more closely involved in the process and is better prepared for their annual performance review.
- **A superior or manager.** This is the most common type of appraisal, so this book will chiefly focus on it. This may involve the employee's direct superior or someone higher up the chain of command.
- **A peer.** This type of appraisal is very useful when evaluating the quality of an employee's work. When an employee's direct superior is not an expert in the field that the employee under evaluation works in, they may bring in another specialist in order to assess the quality of their work. For example, this is common in the publishing and research sectors.
- **A subordinate.** This has the benefit of provi-

ding insight into the employees' view of the corporate hierarchy and their management methods.

- **A client or customer.** This is a useful way of gauging customer satisfaction, as it provides insight into ways that the product or service on offer could be improved.
- **A combination of different evaluators.** 360 degree feedback uses this approach.

360 DEGREE FEEDBACK

360 degree feedback is an approach which uses several indicators to evaluate an employee's capabilities, including their colleagues, their superiors, and sometimes even their clients. All those involved, including the employee, fill out the same questionnaire and comment on the employee's work. All the responses are anonymous, and are used to calculate an average. This kind of appraisal is used to create a fuller, more objective picture than the evaluation provided by traditional methods, and allows the employee to compare their own view of their work with their colleagues' perspectives.

PERFORMANCE EVALUATION

In their article *The Substantive Nature of Job Performance Variability: In Individual Differences and Behavior in Organisations*, the renowned professors Campbell, Gasser and Oswald explain that in order to evaluate one's own performance or the performance of one's subordinates, it is essential to take a global view of all the relevant actions and behaviours within the company. Performance cannot be reduced to the resources used or the results of a certain series of actions; it is about the actions themselves, which attest to the employee's contribution to the company's objectives. Given that results may be influenced by external factors (lack of resources, strained working relationships, unforeseen incidents, etc.), it is important to look beyond them and focus in equal measure on the employee's behaviour and methods.

Campbell et al propose a multifactor model which identifies eight components of performance (the supervision component can be disregarded unless the appraisal is concerned with this kind of activity):

- role-specific skills;
- non-role-specific skills;
- written and oral communication skills;
- effort;
- personal discipline;
- collaboration and contributions to team and colleague performances;
- leadership and supervision skills;
- management and administrative skills.

Below you will find a list of questions relating to each of these factors, which evaluators and employees alike will find useful while preparing for a performance appraisal. Depending on which decisions need to be made and the type of appraisal you are preparing for, some questions may prove more relevant than others.

Specific skills

- **Evaluator:**
  - Which skills have been deemed essential for the employee's role?
  - What behaviours does the employee exhibit in relation to each skill (actions, ideas, or relational attitudes)?
  - What level of proficiency can be associated

with the observed behaviours?
  - What are the employee's strengths and weaknesses?
  - What corrective actions or training could be used to help the employee to improve?
- **Employee:**
  - Which skills are deemed essential for my role?
  - Which situations have given me an opportunity to demonstrate each of my skills? What did I do exactly?
  - How proficient am I in each skill? Am I comfortable putting this skill into practice, no matter the context?
  - What are my strengths and weaknesses?
  - What solutions could I put in place and what training do I need in order to improve?

Non-specific skills

- **Evaluator:**
  - Has the employee participated in activities or projects adjacent to their main role?
  - If so, have they demonstrated other skills in these situations? Which skills? By extension, what behaviours can be identified?

- **Employee:**
  - Which activities and projects have I participated in which fall outside the main responsibilities of my role?
  - What skills was I able to demonstrate on those occasions? In what way?

Communication

- **Evaluator:**
  - In which situations has the employee demonstrated their written and oral communication skills?
  - Which means of communication can they use proficiently? Where is there room for improvement? What suggestions could I make?
- **Employee:**
  - In which situations did I feel like I was demonstrating my communication skills?
  - Which means of communication can I use proficiently? What aspects do I need to improve? How could I improve them?

Supervision

- **Evaluator:**
  - How has the employee contributed to their

subordinates' performance? Which behaviours indicate that their leadership style is appropriate and effective (setting goals, encouraging expected behaviours, imposing appropriate rewards and punishments)? What advice could I offer?

- **Employee:**
  - Which of my actions attest to my leadership skills and my contribution to my subordinates' performance? What are my needs (technical resources, additional staff, conflict resolution training, etc.)?

Management/Administration

- **Evaluator:**
  - Which observable actions and behaviours give an indication of the employee's management skills (aside from those related to direct supervision, as mentioned above)?
  - Did they set appropriate goals?
  - Did they distribute the resources and/or workload appropriately?
  - In administrative terms, have they contributed to the development of the company (by acquiring human, financial, or other

resources)?

- **Employee:**
  - In which situations have I demonstrated my leadership skills?
  - Did I control the way the situation developed?
  - Did I help to resolve problems or crisis situations so that the goals could be achieved?
  - Have I acquired additional resources (secured contracts, generated profits, obtained tools or other resources through a partnership, etc.)?

Effort

- **Evaluator:**
  - Does the employee put effort into their work? Is their effort consistent? Have they gone above and beyond what was required of them? Have they had to work under difficult conditions (periods of stress, pressure, etc.)? What motivates them?
- **Employee:**
  - Have I put enough effort into my work? Have I put consistent effort into my work? Have I gone above and beyond what was required of me? How can I prove it? What motivates me?

Discipline

- **Evaluator:**
  - Have I noticed any negative or counter-productive behaviour such as the consumption of alcohol or illegal substances on the job, rule-breaking, or excessive absenteeism? How can I prove it? How can I broach this subject?
  - TIP: consult the human resources department, the guidance counsellor or a doctor as part of your preparation for addressing this subject.
- **Employee:**
  - Have I been exhibiting negative or counter-productive behaviour which could lead to me being reprimanded during the meeting? What attitude should I adopt if this issue is brought up during the meeting?
  - TIP: if you are struggling with personal problems, talk to them in confidence with someone you trust, your guidance counsellor or the company doctor.

Collaboration

- **Evaluator:**
  - Does the employee help and support their colleagues? Do they work well in teams?
- **Employee:**
  - In which situations have I contributed to my colleagues' performance through effective collaboration, or by providing help and support, etc.?

Example skills evaluation grid

Evaluation of the employee's level of proficiency in various skills, based on concrete observations

<table>
<tr><td colspan="2" align="center">COMMERCIAL PROSPECTION</td></tr>
<tr><td colspan="2">

- has taken a planned, structured approach to prospection
- has identified a new potential client niche
- has correctly identified client needs

</td></tr>
<tr><td>

☐ No experience
☐ Learning
☐ Competent in familiar situations

</td><td>

☐ Competent in unfamiliar situations
☐ Proficient in all situations

</td></tr>
<tr><td colspan="2" align="center">SALES</td></tr>
<tr><td colspan="2">

- has increased their sales figures for classic products
- has contributed to sales growth by suggesting new marketing strategies

</td></tr>
<tr><td>

☐ No experience
☐ Learning
☐ Competent in familiar situations

</td><td>

☐ Competent in unfamiliar situations
☐ Proficient in all situations

</td></tr>
</table>

ADVICE

- has advised clients on the new range of services under supervision from their mentor

☐ No experience	☐ Competent in unfamiliar situations
☐ Learning	
☐ Competent in familiar situations	☐ Proficient in all situations

OTHER SKILLS

☐ No experience	☐ Competent in unfamiliar situations
☐ Learning	
☐ Competent in familiar situations	☐ Proficient in all situations

Setting objectives

It is important to set clear objectives so that a competent employee performs to the best of their ability, and so that their actions are focused in a way that meets the company's expectations. Imagine that two football coaches each just told the players on their teams to kick the ball about a bit. No matter how beautifully they dribbled the ball around, the resulting match would be terribly dull. Conversely, they could motivate their players by giving them the objective of scoring as many goals against the opposing team as possible. This also applies in the office: in order to drive performance up, actions must have meaning and must be aligned with the company's objectives. Whether you are the evaluator or the employee, make sure that each of your actions is in line with the objectives of the company, the team, and your own role by asking yourself the following questions:

- Which objectives for meeting the company's expectations are shared by all employees? What objectives are shared by your team members in terms of putting their strategies into action? What are your individual objectives in terms of meeting expectations at an operational and strategic level? Are your individual objectives compatible with the collective objectives?
- What kinds of results would you like to obtain? Of what nature (product/service)? To what end (profit, mass production, innovation, reputation, collective service, application of legislation, etc.)?

- What factors prove that your objectives are being achieved? How can you measure the gap between your goals and your results?
- How can you gather information (interviews, questionnaires, observation, data analysis, etc.)? How frequently? How much would this cost? Would this information be easily accessible?
- Have you chosen effective, relevant criteria for verifying that your objectives have been achieved? Or should you choose different indicators?

SMART METHOD

The SMART method can be used to set intelligent objectives which can be more easily understood by employees. They should be:

- **(S)** specific, meaning clear and precise so that everyone can understand them;
- **(M)** measurable through the use of indicators, so that you can track your progress;
- **(A)** attainable, though still ambitious enough to be a source of motivation;
- **(R)** realistic, in line with company policy and the employee's role;

- **(T)** time-bound, meaning that they should have a fixed deadline and milestones.

Defining the performance criteria

Various indicators can be used to measure and evaluate performance. According to De Ketele and Roegiers, the evaluation process can be described as "comparing a set of information with a set of (referential) criteria"[1] (*ibid.* p. 33). Just as we use a ruler to measure lengths and a set of scales to weigh objects, managers must first define the relevant criteria according to their company culture. It is equally necessary to establish different indicators for different positions and roles. Ask yourself what you want to evaluate and what criteria should be given priority. For example, use questionnaires to assess customer satisfaction, data analysis to calculate production volume or profit, interviews to evaluate procedural effectiveness, statistics to estimate shortfalls, etc. Indicators are simply points of reference which allow us to estimate the size of the gaps between expected and actual results.

---

1. This quotation has been translated by 50Minutes.com.

According to the professor of work psychology Claude Lévy-Leboyer, there are two types of indicators: objective indicators and subjective indicators. Examples of the former include budget adherence, production estimates, frequency, deadline adherence, error frequency, customer satisfaction levels, product quality, adherence to security measures, etc. However, employees cannot always control all of these factors, so you should always consider how relevant these factors are to the employee's role. During appraisals, subjective indicators tend to be used most often. Those used most frequently include scales which are used to rate employee behaviour:

- **Graphic scales**, as shown below:

Totally
unsatisfactory |........|........|........| satisfactory Very

- **Behaviourally Anchored Rating Scales (BARS)**, in which real behaviours are associated with each level of a rating scale (which should have been developed by experts on the subject). In his book *Évaluation du personnel.*

Quels objectifs ? Quelles méthodes ? ("Personnel Evaluations: Which goals? Which methods?"), Claude Lévy-Leboyer gives an interesting example of the way a bank employee's "client relations" could be evaluated:

Above average performance	Below average performance
"Very attentive when advising clients and dealing with their issues. Always patient and ready to provide any necessary explanations, even with difficult customers. Tries to reduce waiting time at the counter and to go above and beyond to meet customer needs."	"Often causes problems with customers through bad attitudes or incompetence. Acts as though customers do not need to understand our procedures."

- **Behaviour Observation Scales (BOS)**, a version of BARS which also consists of a rating scale, but with more concise descriptions of the behaviour in question at each level. The evaluator then makes a note of how frequently the individual exhibits this behaviour. For example:

Identifies the root causes of customer dissatisfaction
Almost never 1 – 2 – 3 – 4 – 5 Almost always

Listens to customer complaints
Almost never 1 – 2 – 3 – 4 – 5 Almost always

Gauges how important the problem is for the customer
Almost never 1 – 2 – 3 – 4 – 5 Almost always

Asks questions so as to better understand the problem
Almost never 1 – 2 – 3 – 4 – 5 Almost always

ADVICE FOR MANAGERS

- The importance accorded to each criterion should be based on the employee's role. For example, punctuality is an essential quality for those working in business, whereas avoiding errors is more important for an accountant.
- As well as varying according to the

employee's profession, the importance of each criterion will also be influenced by the context and the objectives of the company and sector in question. For example, the financial services sector has very different goals (growth, profit, etc.) from the social services sector (resource allocation, project relevance, quality of relationships, etc.).

- The company's priorities will evolve over time: in ten years they will not necessarily be identical to current priorities. You should readjust your chosen indicators on a regular basis and pay attention to their contextual relevance.
- Do not forget that you are evaluating individuals who are constantly evolving. It is often wise to use different performance indicators depending on whether you are evaluating a new recruit or an experienced employee.

In addition to criteria targeted at analysing processes and results, you should also consider motivation. The motivational factors that act as a driving force in your company may include shared values, stability, salary, training opportunities, career advancement opportunities and independence, among others. Consider what factors should be maintained or adjusted in order to keep motivation strong. It is also important for each employee to define their own motivational criteria and for the evaluator to pay attention to them so that they can ensure that their team remains focused.

PERFORMANCE APPRAISALS 101

The basics

In order to build up a sense of respect and trust and to create a safe environment, you should always inform the employee who is due to be evaluated of the following aspects of the meeting in advance:

- **The date, time, place and duration of the appraisal.** The employee should be informed of the meeting around a fortnight in advance so that they can prepare to the best of their ability.
- **The methods and resources which can be used to prepare** (are there self-evaluation

forms or templates to fill in?).

- **The purpose of the appraisal** within the context of the company as a whole.
- **The subject of the appraisal:** the skills related to their role and/or team performance, working methods, achievements, critical incidents, behaviour on the job, etc.
- **The means of evaluation:** rating scales, observation scales, or another frame of reference.
- **The structure of the appraisal** and the different stages involved.

ADVICE FOR EMPLOYERS

- Schedule the meeting at a time when the company will not be busy so that your own judgement will not be clouded by external factors and to ensure that the meeting takes place in a calm environment.
- Do not catch anyone off guard by leaving it until the day before to inform them of the meeting, as this approach can stir up resentment.
- Use a neutral location where you will not be disturbed.
- Prepare yourself mentally so that you are

> in the best mood possible, and adopt a positive attitude.
> - Set aside some extra time (1 h to 1 h 30) in case the employee has any questions or comments.

Preparation

The success of the meeting largely depends on how well both participants prepare for it, so its effectiveness will be greatly diminished if either the employee or the evaluator shows up unprepared. In order to establish a constructive dialogue, both parties should bear the performance criteria that will be used in mind while preparing (cf. Performance evaluation). There are several documents that can be used at this stage of the process:

- Written information about the employee (thank you letters, complaint forms, service notes, etc.).
- Informational documents or graphs (absence statistics, results charts, etc.).
- The employee's CV.
- The performance appraisal from the previous

year (if applicable).
- The employee's self-evaluation (to be completed by them before the meeting).
- The evaluation chart for the present year. The manager will fill it in during the meeting, and can provide the employee with a blank copy before the meeting so that they are aware of the skills that will be evaluated and prepare their arguments.

Step by step

Once you have prepared, it will be time to get stuck in. But how do these infamous performance appraisals actually work? The following table could prove useful, whether you are the evaluator or the employee:

DISCUSSION OF THE OBJECTIVES FOR THE COMING YEAR	
Actions	• Overview of the company's general goals. • Definition and adjustment of individual goals using the SMART method.
Who?	The manager, followed by dialogue between both parties to define individual objectives
DEFINITION OF CAREER OBJECTIVES	
Actions	• Discussion of the employee's professional ambitions (opportunities for promotion, training, transfer, etc.)
Who?	Both parties
OTHER QUESTIONS	
Actions	• Discussion of various problems observed within the company: atmosphere, overwork, etc.
Who?	The employee

END OF THE INTERVIEW	
Actions	• Check that all the necessary issues have been addressed. • Sum up the decisions made during the course of the interview regarding corrective actions and new objectives. • Go over each participant's commitments and short-term follow-up measures. • Schedule a follow-up meeting. • Both parties sign the evaluation form as proof of agreement.
Who?	Both parties

Ideally, the meeting should end with both sides coming to a "win-win" agreement, but unfortunately this is not always possible. However, this does not necessarily make the meeting a failure; take a step back and focus on the positive.

> To sum up, the appraisal is about clarification, communication, motivation, development, responsibility, finding meaning and value.

TOP TIPS

FOR THE EVALUATOR

- **Put the employee at ease.** The first seconds of the interview are important and set the tone for what comes next. This means that you should:
  - welcome them in a friendly manner (ask them how their holidays were, if they had a good weekend, etc.);
  - shake their hand;
  - smile and adopt an open attitude;
  - invite them to sit down;
  - keep to the company's dress code (shirt and tie, etc.) as a sign of respect;
  - use a tone that is neither overly warm nor overly aggressive.
- **Ask the employee questions** to keep the dialogue going:

When broaching a sensitive subject	"And what is your opinion?" "What do you think about this subject?"
When they mention something that surprises you or which you want to discuss in more depth	"Really?" "What do you mean?" "What criteria are you basing that on?" "Could you give an example?" "To what extent?" "What do you understand by that?"
If you are not certain about something	"How did this come about?" "What led you to make this decision or to act in this way?"
When they state an opinion	"What made you think that…?"

| Source: Barrier, G. (2013) *Les langages du corps en relation d'aide. La communication non verbale au-delà des mots*. Paris: ESF. p. 26.

- **Value your employees in order to motivate them.** Robert Eisenberger, a psychology professor at the University of Houston, and

Dr. Florence Stinglhamber, a specialist in psychological science, have carried out several studies focused on valuing employees rather than devaluing them. Internal surveys showed that employees are more or less aware of how much the company and their superiors value their contributions. The support that they feel they are receiving influences their wellbeing, their engagement and their performance at work, among other factors. Never forget that while you are evaluating your employee, they will be evaluating you at the same time. Recognise their contributions, show interest in them, and congratulate them. The more your employees feel like they and their work are appreciated, the more committed they will be. Try to use expressions like: "I noticed that you did…", "Thank you for doing…", "Good job on the clarity of that dossier you submitted…", "You have really improved in terms of sales, I have received excellent feedback from clients x and y", "Thank you for helping Mark to close that case yesterday evening…" and so on. More broadly speaking, do not forget to give your employees positive feedback even outside of performance appraisals.

- **Choose your words wisely!** Joseph A. DeVito, Giles Chassé and Carole Vézeau, the authors of *La Communication interpersonnelle* ("Interpersonal Communication"), recommend:
  - talking about situations rather than people: for example, saying things like "there was" instead of "you did not";
  - keeping your criticism positive: for example, saying "I prefer the second version" rather than "this version is no good";
  - using constructive criticism: for example, saying "you should revise the structure of your report so that it is easier to understand" rather than "your writing is terrible";
  - being careful with sensitive subjects: for example, saying "why not edit down this article and remove a few passages so that it reads more fluidly" instead of "your article is too long";
  - being precise: for example, saying "your conclusions are too vague, they should be formulated more clearly" rather than "you have done a bad job".

HOW SHOULD YOU REACT TO AN EMOTIONAL EMPLOYEE?

- Be empathetic.
- Avoid repressing their emotions by saying things like "Don't cry", "Don't get worked up over that", "Don't be upset, it isn't that bad", "Don't worry, you'll be promoted eventually", etc.
- Listen and do not talk about yourself (for example, "I've been in a similar position...").
- Ask them about how they are feeling: "Are there any other things you would like to discuss together?", "Would you like to talk about it?", "Why are you upset?" etc.

FOR THE EMPLOYEE

- **Make sure that you have fully understood the aim of the meeting**. The appraisal's focus will dictate what decisions are taken at the end of it, so it is fundamental to engage with the process: evaluate your skills to give yourself direction, establish your role and any necessary adjustments to be made to it, determine your performance level and your eligibility for a bonus or a promotion, etc.

- **Prepare**. Take the time to reflect on your skills, your achievements, the difficulties you have encountered and the solutions you could put forward, the sensitive issues you would like to address and ways of phrasing them constructively.
- **Be responsive during the interview**. Although one of your superiors will be evaluating you, this does not mean that you should remain passive. Be proactive by expressing your ideas and suggesting solutions, as engaging with the appraisal will attest to your motivation. If you are quite introverted, you could write a message for your evaluator and ask them to take it into account.
- **Work on your body language**. Make eye contact with your evaluator, sit up straight and do not slouch, keep your head up, and be confident. If you feel stressed, try to take deep breaths and do not gesticulate wildly. Finally, do not get too close to the evaluator while speaking, although you should also avoid creating too much distance between you. Finding the right balance will help the dialogue to flow

more easily.

- **Do not wallow in confusion**. If you have not understood something that the evaluator has said, ask them to repeat or rephrase it. Do not leave the meeting until you have fully grasped all of their conclusions, as they will be crucial for what comes next.
- **Avoid criticising your colleagues**. Express your feelings about the situation and describe the behaviour that is causing problems. For example, "It bothers me when Nadine turns the radio on in the office because it affects my concentration. I would like to talk about it. Do you have any advice?" Of course, the best solution is to speak to those involved directly.

A WINNING ATTITUDE

The Pygmalion effect, which was discovered by Robert Rosenthal (American psychologist, born in 1933), is a phenomenon whereby an individual's chances of success can be increased when they internalise positive beliefs about their own skills. This self-fulfilling prophecy means that by imagining your own success, you will then unconsciously adopt the behaviour which will allow you to achieve your goal.

The opposite effect is known as the golem effect. For example, if you are convinced that the meeting will go badly, this will lead you to adopt a negative attitude throughout it and your initial fears will become reality.

FAQS

HOW FREQUENTLY SHOULD PERFORMANCE APPRAISALS BE HELD?

Many companies hold performance appraisals once a year, although it is up to the managers and human resources personnel to decide what would be best and most effective for the company. Consider organising a few shorter meetings throughout the year to familiarise your employees with the process, as this will make it easier for them to communicate with you, negate some of the dread that can be associated with performance appraisals and leave you better equipped to reorient the team, if necessary.

HOW CAN I ENSURE THAT THE ATMOSPHERE OF THE MEETING FOSTERS COMMUNICATION AND TRUST?

To foster an atmosphere of trust in the meeting,

you should adopt the right attitude on a daily basis rather than just the night before; it takes time and effort to build trust. In their article *Les Comportements suscitant la confiance des subordonnés. Un examen de trois déterminants possibles* ("Behaviours which foster trust with subordinates: An examination of three possible determinants"), the psychology researchers Annick Ebacher, Danielle Desbiens and Roland Foucher studied this issue and identified various behaviours which should be practised in order to win the trust of your subordinates: consistency, integrity, keeping your promises, availability, competence, loyalty, fairness, discretion, openness, receptiveness, provision of accurate information, sharing, delegation of power and feedback. Try to work on several of these behaviours in order to build trust with your teams. Creating an atmosphere built on trust affects employee satisfaction, results, commitment to innovative processes, behaviour and willingness to interact with you. Slim Lambert, the author of *Les Secrets du leader manager idéal* ("The Secrets to Becoming the Ideal Leader and Manager"), has drawn up a list of tips you can use to foster trust:

- never reveal confidential information;
- never use your colleagues as scapegoats for your own mistakes;
- be fair and avoid favouritism;
- seek people out and take the time to make small talk;
- praise successful efforts at the first opportunity;
- get involved in day-to-day matters which are unrelated to your role as a supervisor: wish your employees a happy birthday, discuss ways of making the office more comfortable with them, contribute to funds for birthday or baby gifts, etc.;
- remember that everyone makes mistakes and help your employees to reflect on the matter and redirect their efforts, if necessary.

CAN I TALK ABOUT ANYTHING DURING THE MEETING?

A performance appraisal is a time for dialogue, and the participants should be able to bring up any issues they are struggling with. The following topics are all perfectly appropriate:

- the objectives which represent the expectations of the manager, employee, clients, etc. within the company;

- achievements and failures: this is not a question of judging the other person, but rather of analysing anything which does not work and the reasons behind these failures in order to put effective solutions in place;
- training or resources which are needed to maintain and improve performance;
- motivation, salary and career opportunities;
- conflicts, misunderstandings and any other problems related to wellbeing (poor work environment, overwork, malfunctioning equipment, etc.).

HOW SHOULD I REACT TO A NEGATIVE PERFORMANCE APPRAISAL?

Whether or not you feel satisfied after your performance appraisal, you should view it from a constructive angle. In order to show that you are "solution-oriented", prepare some ideas ahead of time by imagining solutions you could suggest during the appraisal in order to improve results. By acting as a problem solver, you will project a strong image of yourself, which the evaluator will be appreciated and which will be rewarding for you. Identifying obstacles, analysing approaches and finding solutions can often be as important as the results themselves. Whether you are the evaluator or the employee, the IDEAL model can often shed light on any spanners in the works:

	IDEAL Model	Questions to determine what is blocking the problem-solving process
I	**Identify** the problems	Has the person identified the problems facing them?
D	**Define** and describe the problem	Has the person correctly defined the problems, in accordance with the views of the company and their other teammates?
E	**Explore** possible strategies	Has the person explored alternatives in sufficient depth?
A	**Act** according to those strategies	Has the person formulated an action plan?
L	**Look back** and evaluate the effects of your actions	Has the person evaluated the effects of their actions?

| Source: Bransford, J.D. and Stein, B.S. (1984) *The Ideal Problem Solver: A Guide For Improving Thinking, Learning and Creativity.* Wallingford: W.H. Freeman and Company. p.12.

Case study

Aline organises training for her colleagues in order to keep them apprised of adjustments to company regulations. She spends a lot of time preparing her presentation, and in particular, she creates a Prezi (a presentation-making tool similar to PowerPoint) to make it more dynamic. The day before her appraisal, she gets the chance to show off her skills. When the other participants share their opinions, Aline's face falls. On the whole, they are dissatisfied: they were left unimpressed by the Prezi, which they found confusing, and do not feel as though the training has left them prepared to put the new regulations into practice.

On the day of the performance appraisal, Aline's manager, who has heard of the fiasco, is surprised by her apparently indifferent attitude so soon after this failure. During the interview, Aline makes her position clear by saying, "I'm sure you've heard that the training for the new regulations was a failure. I've put a lot of thought into adapting my approach, and I'd like to take this chance to discuss it with you." Although she had initially planned to prove her teaching skills, in the end it is Aline's talent for problem-solving that impresses her supervisor.

What happened? (IDEAL approach)

I – Immediately after the training session, Aline

set out to identify the elements of the training which were seen as inadequate by analysing the evaluation forms and asking some of the participants.

D – She defined the problem, and concluded that it stemmed from an issue with the training method.

E – She explored other possibilities by asking those around her and by doing some online research.

A – She put a plan into action and decided to choose a presentation method better suited to the content. She also reviewed the pace of the sessions and developed various exercises to allow the participants to absorb the new infor-mation through practice.

L – After giving a demo of the new presentation in front of two colleagues and receiving positive feedback, she feels ready to face her audience again.

HOW SHOULD I HANDLE AN EMPLOYEE WHO REACTS BADLY TO ANY KIND OF CRITICISM?

André Guittet, the author of *L'entretien. Techniques et practiques* ("Interview Techniques and Practices"), suggests taking the following approaches when dealing with various difficult attitudes. Note that these terms are labels coined by the author and do not refer to psychiatric diagnoses.

- **Paranoia:** do not get into debates or try to justify the decisions that were made, and stand firm.
- **Deviance:** keep your thoughts and feelings to yourself, stick to the facts and let them say their piece.
- **Anxiety:** put them at ease by praising them and encouraging them.
- **Irascibility:** avoid direct confrontation by reminding them of the rules or openly challenging their suggestions, and channel their emotions productively.
- **Narcissism:** let them speak, then set boundaries and explain what is and is not acceptable.

- **Hysteria:** keep your cool and stay objective so that they are more likely to calm down.
- **Obsession:** present your arguments gradually and give them time to reflect on the evidence you have gathered.
- **Depression:** put things into perspective and help them to do the same.

HOW CAN I IDENTIFY THE OBSTACLES TO THE GOALS SET DURING THE PERFORMANCE APPRAISAL AND HELP OTHERS TO OVERCOME THEM?

Our lives are a series of successes and failures which collectively define our existence and influence our behaviour. The American psychologist Taibi Kahler (born in 1943), building on the work of Eric Berne (Canadian psychiatrist, 1910-1970), the founder of transactional analysis, explains that our actions are linked to five restrictive messages, which he called "drivers": "Be perfect", "Be strong", "Hurry up", "Please others" and "Try hard". Once internalised, these messages influence our attitudes and create obstacles which can come in different forms. The two situations below provide a good illustration of this process:

- **Be perfect**. Alexander is very organised, and when he began the project of launching a company newspaper, he swiftly put his supervisor at ease by planning everything down to the finest details. However, the final version was delayed by several weeks before it was published. What happened? Why did he not stick to the deadlines in the end? During the appraisal, his supervisor asked him about it, and discovered that the restrictive message "Be perfect" had taken hold of Alexander. He had spent the last few weeks compulsively rereading the final copy after his perfectionism eclipsed and took priority over his time management.
- **Please others**. The director entrusted his subordinate, Lauren, to write an urgent article for the end of the week. Despite having planned to take time off, she proved flexible and postponed her holiday so as to meet the new goals. In exchange, her manager temporarily reassigned all of her other responsibilities so that she could concentrate on writing the article. However, on Friday evening, Lauren

is left sitting in front of her computer, filled with frustration because she is still a long way from finishing her work. What happened? In fact, she helped George move boxes out of the archives, comforted Julie after her break-up, photocopied some files for Claire, and so on. After trying to please everyone and putting others before herself, Lauren was unable to achieve her goal.

Alternative messages which give "permission" to act in another way can be used to overcome these restrictive messages and resolve the situation.

Driver	Permission
Be perfect	"You have the right to make mistakes."
Be strong	"You have the right to feel emotions."
Hurry up	"You have the right to take your time."
Please others	"You have the right to live according to your own values (instead of other people's) and to make yourself happy."
Try hard	"You have the right to concentrate on your own goals and to limit your focus."

Given that appraisals are the perfect time to delegate responsibilities and to set individual goals, you can also use them as a chance to take advantage of the benefits of this method. For example, try entrusting urgent tasks to people who respond to the driver "hurry up", delicate tasks to those who are sensitive to "be perfect", projects that require tenacity to those who lean towards "be strong", and so on. As an employee,

OVER TO YOU

SELF-EVALUATION EXERCISE

In order to prepare effectively for your performance appraisal, try asking yourself the following questions. They will guide you as you reflect and will help you to construct your arguments, to identify your future goals and the problems you encountered over the previous year, and so on.

Current position

- What are the main responsibilities of your position?
- Which of your duties do you enjoy most and which bore you?
- Have your duties changed in the last period?

Major events during the relevant period

- Which work-related events do you believe have had a significant impact on your actions? Did they play a positive or negative role?

Activity overview

- Have you improved your skills and knowledge during this period?
- Have you have access to the resources you needed in order to develop your skills?
- Are you satisfied with your results?
- What helped or hindered you in achieving your goals?

Skills and improvement

- Which skills and abilities do you believe to be most important for your position?
- Which skills and knowledge could you improve?
- Would you like to embark on training to develop certain skills?

Objectives for the year ahead

- What are your main professional goals at an individual and collective level?
- What consequences will these goals have for your position, for your team, for the company, etc.?
- What are your career ambitions? Would you like to transfer to a different position? To take on more responsibilities? Or slow down?

We want to hear from you!
Leave a comment on your online library
and share your favourite books on social media!

FURTHER READING

BIBLIOGRAPHY

- Barrier, G. (2013) *Les langages du corps en relation d'aide. La Communication non verbale au-delà des mots.* Paris: ESF.

- Bransford, J. D. and Stein, B. S. (1984) *The Ideal Problem Solver: Guide For Improving Thinking, Learning and Creativity.* Wallingford: W. H. Freeman and Company. p. 12.

- Campbell, J. P., Gasser, M. B. and Oswald, F. L. (1996) The Substantive Nature of Job Performance Variability. Murphy, K. R. ed. *Individual Differences and Behavior in Organizations.* San Francisco: Jossey-Bass Publishers.

- Cardon, A., Lenhardt, V. and Nicolas, P. (2003) *L'analyse transactionnelle.* 2nd edition. Paris: Éditions d'Organisation.

- De Ketele, J. and Roegiers, X. (2009) *Méthodologie du recueil d'informations. Fondement des méthodes d'observation, de questionnaire, d'interview et d'études de documents.* 4th edition. Brussels: De Boeck.

- DeVito, J. A., Chassé, G. and Vézeau, C. (2001) *La communication interpersonnelle.* Montréal:

Pearson ERPI.

- Ebacher, A., Desbiens, D. and Foucher R. (2003) Les comportements suscitant la confiance des subordonnés. Un examen de trois déterminants possibles. *Évaluation et développement des compétences au travail.* Louvain-La-Neuve: Presses universitaires de Louvain. pp. 361-369.

- Eisenberger, R. and Stinglhamber, F. (2011) *Perceived Organizational Support: Fostering Enthusiastic and Productive Employees.* Washington: Magination Press (American Psychological Association).

- Granger, R. (2015) Méthode SMART. *Manager Go.* [Online]. [Accessed 25 October 2017]. Available from: <http://www.manager-go.com/vente/methode-smart.htm>

- Guittet, A. (2008) *L'entretien. Techniques et pratiques.* Paris: Armand Colin.

- Idem commercial. (No date) *Fonctionnement.* [Online]. [Accessed 25 October 2017]. Available from: <http://www.idem-commercial.com/page/1472_process_com_comportement_sous_stress_taibi_kahler_profil_de_personnalite_stress_besoin_psychologique_communication_motivation_perseverant_promoteur_empathique_rebelle_travaillomane_reveur.php>

- Jacquet, S. (No date) Le leadership : un état personnel, des capacités ou une réelle intelligence situationnelle ? Présentation des grands courants d'explication du leadership. *CREG*. [Online]. [Accessed 25 October 2017]. Available from: <http://www.creg.ac-versailles.fr/IMG/pdf/leardership.pdf>

- Jussim, L. (1986) Self-Fulfilling Prophecies: A Theoretical and Integrative Review. *Psychological Review*. 93(4), pp. 429-445.

- Jussim, L. and Harber, K. D. (2005) Teacher Expectations and Self-Fulfilling Prophecies: Knowns and Unknowns, Resolved and Unresolved Controversies. *Personality and Social Psychology Review*. 9(2).

- Lambert, S. (2006) *Les secrets du leader manager ideal*. Paris: Vuibert.

- Lévy-Leboyer, C. (2007) *Évaluation du personnel. Quels objectifs ? Quelles méthodes ?* 6th edition. Paris: Éditions d'Organisation.

- Lévy-Leboyer, C. (2007) *Le 360 °. Outil de développement personnel*. Paris: Éditions d'Organisation.

- Medef. (2015) *L'entretien annuel d'évaluation : mode d'emploi*. [Online]. [Accessed 25 October 2017]. Available from: <http://www.medef-rh.fr/L-en-tretien-annuel-d-evaluation-mode-d-emploi_a251.html>

- Motiv RV. (No date) *Les 6 types de personnalité dans la méthode Process communication*. [Online]. [Accessed 25 October 2017]. Available from:<http://www.motivrh-formation.com/

les-6-types-de-personnalite-dans-le-modele-pro-
cess-communication>

- Stewart, I. and Joines, V. (2000) *Manuel d'analyse transactionnelle*. Paris: InterÉditions.

- Zacharis, P. (No date) *Les styles de leadership selon Hersey et Blanchard*. [Online]. [Accessed 25 October 2017]. Available from: <http://www.patrickzacharis.be/les-styles-de-leadership-selon-hersey-et-blanchard/>

History
Business
Coaching
Book Review
Health & Wellbeing

50MINUTES.com

ISHIKAWA DIAGRAM
Anticipate and solve problems within your business

Material Method Machine
Mother Nature Measure Men

THE BATTLE OF AUSTERLITZ

NETWORKING

IMPROVE YOUR GENERAL KNOWLEDGE
IN A BLINK OF AN EYE !

www.50minutes.com